IBLT with the Missing Party at the Party

Ideal Bouquet Lickinness Taste: An Ancient Alien Fighting Technique

by

Tye Wildncool

RoseDog Books
PITTSBURGH, PENNSYLVANIA 15238

RoseDog Books
585 Alpha Drive, Suite 103
Pittsburgh, PA 15238
Visit our website at *www.rosedogbookstore.com*

ISBN: 979-8-89341-886-6
eISBN: 979-8-88812-822-0

An Outer Space Spy Love Mystery Party

This is a story into the future, concerning two main couples; Ideal Taste- GSB (get smart bond) or agent 00786 and his lady Uzona Peach, and their friend Kandyer Stir- agent 00867 and his lady Sugarcream. As a pizza delivery man Ideal gets tak'in to Outerspace by an all women crew of a Mining spaceship, getting lost and ending up on the unknown habitable planet Zon and L.I.P. (lost in place) He is also in a Band with Kandyer, Soaro, and El D Vapor. The rest of the band take Off to outerspace to find Ideal and end up L.I.P. at Zon also, I'm doing Big Things. Also with famed JT 48 (Forebe) and Middle Agents (females).

Comes with theory in groups of Fives

From Summer "86"

Summer 86

520 3.6.06

Prepair Title

12   26   00   2000

4:24   4.20   .2020

2. Air   3. Earth   4. Fire   5. Water

With the addition of a fifth element;   M.O.P.   ZAZ   14y   11d   23h

S_p_a_c_e_

We can become part of the Universe.

Ideal Taste with Sweet Roll.   10:54 p.7.24.22   9-17-20

Missing Party at the Party

By Tye Wildncool

10 Years in the Baking

Don't drink all the fountain of youth we have various power plants, delicious.

The Lovener   1247p   2.7.19   T.W.

He was a Spy that get's High   TIMES N DATES

Lovely's Lover   8:52.12.31.19p

Sweeterness inside Outerspace Innerspace and other Space

The Reality of a Reality with a Reality

Respect-Protect-Detect-Reflect-Interject

pic

Magnetic   Rush   Fit   Connect   Theory

Kake n Bake

5W   4F   3E   2A   IS

Lift off 1

Pre-Pair

High

The Texture of Creation; The Theory groups of Fives.

Heaven - Politics - God - Jehovah – Elders - 24

Paradise - Medical - Lord - Jesus - Disciples - 12

Fraternal TWINS   Witnesses   1.Comforter   2nd.Counselor

Eden - Magic - Rules - Holy Spirit - Joe - Spirits - 7

Garden of Eden - Love - Law - Holy Ghost - Rick -Guards - 4

The Valley - Life - Army - The Mystery - Mike - Angels - 2

Devil

Antichrist

False Prophet

666

616

M.O.P. Movie Outline Project

It began like a good dream after smok'in the best of Bud, then some nightmares!

Ideal (the Spy) and his friends, Kandyer Stir, Soaro, and El D Vapor we're the B.S. (Band in Space) At this time definitely B.S. (Banned in Space), then to become actors B.S. (Behind the Scenes), there Are episodes of different T.V. shows, like the O.S.M. (On the Side of your Mind) show. The local Pizzaman turns up missing, tak'in to space by an all women crew of a mining spaceship. There's Secret agent GSB (Get Smart Bond) or 00786 (Ideal), Licky Love, ShadeShadow, and Dark Diamond (Kandyer Stir) or agent 00867, at the Party at Vallyhill the UPHOLDOFF BE-HOLDON Relish! The crew With Ideal, and the band following, all get L.I.P. (lost in place). Accidentally finding a habitable planet And stranded stay temporarily, comes with theory.

FURTHER
N
FARTHER
With ENGLISH AFTERMATH
VITAMINS & DENNER ROLLS
VANILLA SWEET ROLL

Sugar Dish Castle with it's stage, music, and seating areas, kitchen building in the back, skyway Connected to the bedroom building, along the side this connected, also skyway wize to the East Wing (building above the theater), with various security towers, including entry area. There's the coffee Building: where the Pink Peach which holds the Smelly Roach cafe and the movement of motion to Emotion in Sunlight Teased Breezes Heat, also the Burngarden, and the Tower of the Sexy Fish. The Castle was built on the planet Zan and eventually shipped, and rebuilt on Earth.

In a strange sort of Tipsy Topsy Turvy way does Ideal do his thing, which is changing identity from a Friendly high to come at the right time, to a specifically mellow spy, or a musician and capable actor.

Degree Frequency

Range Amount

Discern

THE

TRIP

Nougat of

The

GRAND DEZIGNED

Put it over there where we can get to it from anywhere up high, to see the sky, so we can try, the Thing to do to do the thing.

There is Something

In the Side of Your Mind

Is It On Your Side

Presenting with Christmas time favorite

SUGAR BELL RING

Given from

Zap Cookies

SUN

GALAXY

STAR

MOON

IRIDESCENCE

By BANANANANA

Space, finally the Frontier

Illogical?

*

BEEF BREAK CRUMBALIZER EXPORTS

I FORGOT AN THOUGHT ABOUT I.T.

Glissoned Tone:

From the Peace Desk at OLDER & YOUNG

This soon to be true story is based on true possibilitys, the O'le trick door ploy with the Prayer Shuttle, somewhere in the bracket of the Rizidualant valued J-4B-T.

Magic!

Simular to Father O'Blimeys Beau Bell story "Cinderetta"

Sometime before the Day, it was up in the Bush Mountains of Micro City, Ideal and Kandyer were Studying Holy men come to sanctify Holy ground of the sanctuary, it was the morning of the night at the upper yard gate and Ideal was preforming a Prefunktional Pulse absorbing angle snag he forgets and spaces: Ua Ba By Ty Tu, OK no wicked thing will ever cross that threshold again!

Hay that was the Rite for a Resurrection!

Ya mean he's com'in not go'in, take! off! Wait, I wan'na light up first!

Not a Burro?

Not a Burro a lefty, try it they say it's like a pack of Burros! BoOM! Tower Gold Apriscotchbutter From Aquapuco!

Holy Smoke!

I've forgotten half the story as I wrote, the other half I haven't bothered to write, good luc' This 5 part movie maker will captivate the kids, save your animal from constant petting, who knows?

Sometime in the nearest future: D-PIZZA...in Outerspace with whats that house band, EnLO?

Devine*Miraculous*Special*Tough*Good, it's hard to navigate at the speed of sight but we can do it! At Cube.

Pineapple morning...Exactly

From Mince, The Same Different Coin Co.

The Warranty:

This story is a Broad Not General Tale! As you read this complex story, a movie will appear On the Side of Your mind, you may begin to sing, if the movie plays more than four days call a Doctor immediately><><if you cannot read, DO NOT ATTEMPT as you will not understand the words?

Thanks for listening in the Mind, I guess you call yours that, please don't stop in the middle! If you do stop in the middle, you will need to please go back to the beginning due to the threat of Possible short term memory loss, remember?

Garden Eaters & Moon Stone Inc.

Found by a not

Log- Unnoticed: somewhere in Galaxy Spiral 7

Marked: Planet Tunea

Log- Found recently- Assisted: Comborus notification

Marked: Tuneataters

A Theory of my Relativity, BROUGTH TO YOU by,

Rendering

Colognes & Perfumes

The Brunch Munch in the Rendering by Reservation only.

Somewhere in sometime, "We're going into the woid Capt."

"Snazzy! Back to work! Back to the Liquid Food Money Drug Sex chargettic!"

It was four years ago, on this very night; In he's gone! Knowing of on their best!

There was ALF-(Ability Level Food), good action interplay stuff,-or Dark Diamond

in _Bebiched__ with his Fuizhsion Gam Gun. And the Tension Drama_ THE SHADE

OF THE SUNLIGHT__ as you read between the lines you more experienced readers

will in turn see this book*

This view, from the tower of the Sexy Fish.

Printed; A Blueberry_Bubblegum production.

3055509p

00786-; or GSB {get smart bond) derived from; The time agent 00769 had bout

stuck to a banister being fixed with that adhesive, Smart Bond, at the time he was

standing there admiring Nicole Wampuma up on the step ladder of the book

shelves when he was first to about meet her.

******8:17.4..17.17///1.0:47.12.26.00///"86"///5:27.9.6.06\\\"10Y"7M"110"2

H"50m/\<><>\»******

SECOND PAIR 1-5

The RESINATUOS

(a HISTORY OF Ideal Taste)

It was the summer Solstice, the launch lit up the night sky like the shimmering diamond of a stylist.

Tranqualizing Accelerators Zat Man! (Ideal)

(This is the Story of Another World! ZON, Where, do you take plastic mostly means or equals a Barrel of assorted used plastics! And Birds big as various small amusement parks! With similarity's To Teradactal, Golden-Fronted Leaf Bird, Java Rice Bird, Roller, Emerald Cockoo, Pink-Necked Fruit Dove, And Cock of the Rock! (South American)).

There is a great deal of peace on Zon, There they have employed the traditional "Forward men till ya See the Whites of their Red eyes' system! - the Advent and Plasmic war way - mirroring Candy Top The major capital city of Planet TUNEA (fairly near Zon), With the Tuneataters who care what you think, The basic over-seer's of the Universe, often the First Aids and Group Two were in to it as it were and Used to fight the harsh Reefer ways of the Tuneataters, the monitors of Speed Weight Relation and Function.

This is the Party story, some think it may have started even before Light, it does seem to be a night Activity! To this day, so Light'in it Up!

4:20 9.15.08

This Tale will change the World, and the Word, then someday at sometime we may recover. Let us Pay>.   -the Attributation-

TO; THE UPHOLDOFF

From: FIRE ELECTRIC LIGHTNING MINDS of ULTRAVIOLENCE

Edit- 4:20a 5.5.22

0001

The Year: One Hundred Thousands and One

2101AD

The Bud and Beyond. Want Love Need Have Be Feel Voice Touch Sight Thought, Calm Cat, Yes Kandyer. Ideal said as he was passing up smorgasbord pizza pies one then another, like

Lookers, Ideal was look'in for the right stuff, sort of like his love life. Do you see the naturally Artificial flavor drinks?

No thank god! Med Pep Man is gonna sing a song:

Dark Light

So Happy Yer Sad

So Happy Yer Sad

Dark Light

Alright Lefty a shadow shadower where freedom and effort= substance and choice Decision, Paying attention from whence dis appear.

Tremendo version

Be careful with the Bong you'll blow yer head off! We've had another launch! Potato positioned, Dug in, skyless cloud shadow sun ray angle alignment bond!

0002

Hi Miss Wampuma, get 00169's report to 00786 who has recently changed his number.

What that yes to bad about changing from 00769.

He was protecting his identity!

1. Capt. Somethings eating the crew
2. Who? How many?
1. Its about the vacuum of space.
2. Is that where they come from?
1. What will we find?
2. Whats happening!?

The ladies of a certain mineral freighter, forget an space, lost n spaced specified Lessons in Spacing.

They make an unscheduled delivery at D-Pizza, booking another they don't know they'll make?

Memo from SPYC: from Wampuma-The Psychophysical place area grade, the Pattern Symbols Dept. "The Way of Love has Not Control" The Thurmulat SPYC club!

There was an irremoved feel in the air ducts or there bouts, the freighter crew of women And Ideal Taste (the pizza man). They took him past out an suited up for a short trip, supposedly.

No need sending this to manipulations there was more about this in Sex Blame it on Drugs 101 class!, Everyone got Baked Noodles with Tasty Shroom Button Bean dip at the joint in the breeze (planet Zon). It's Pretentious amazement an ambiguity, a turn-on out of the in: Diversment!

Cube's mine launch an crew is still missing. Elsewhere in headlines vanishing Pizza man is still Missing last seen at the space center over a month ago. And in breaking news a satellite telescope pies up and checks out a shimmer (spaceship Craft of the band caught in an ion storm) in a star area which leads to discovery of 1st habitable planet...Just in, for the deductive news segment, Craft, they too are reported lost after their request mission for Most One, J.T., the pizza man we reported on earlier, he's believed to have been abducted by- What's that? As you know today space is quite a place we're everywhere! Apparently he's ended up there without a trace, more later.

Upon hearing the news the King of Earth called his wizard, summon the Agent to find the Guardian to get the Planner to Condition a theory to stabilize! Robotically compute the visual and Audio for Existential (self), Situational (environment), Normative (law), Perceptual (systematic), and The Conceptual (scholastic). Then check Space Wind Earth Fire Water and you'll find the Most one Rhodium Gold Platinum Palladium silver!

Station Two

(couples, Zon, 4B (forebe)

Posh Lumber Party at Vallyhill, JT adventures to spur: Ideal Taste's 69 Moods and Dishes, Concocting forms of famous Mood Dishes or 4B, a conscious subconscious mind feeling, an Atmospherical shimmer! For Privacy Focus: THCBS (Trip High Cartoons Buzz Stone), or Fantasinaddic Congerationable Jungle Plants Kandyer Stir with Ideal Taste!, up to in feel so slow with a loose be down at the tight fast on, the Beholdon!, you've reached the most inner thoughts of my mind, an innerspace place. Station Two when Stationing with sideboar pool (pipe n reefer) 4B, sponge feed at your own risk! All a part of stationing, it's ok not to know just don't forget! The Coco island Lovecloud in Vallyhill, the challenge to be as to.

They searched for the right mixture element elements. Debating over various plants, when Testing one, they discovered this one had a mixture all it's own! Sort of like a secret advantage! While testing one was heard to say I think I'm gonna die, no I'm never gonna Die!

Taste's IDEAL TASTE B.S. (band in space) was troubled, their created Riff Riffs were to much And got them B.S. (banned in space), not being a Band in Space (B.S.) anymore, or no B.S. they were Feeling let down! Banned in all Space, where they couldn't play a place, nor for any Race. It was time for Acting!

(Ideal) Detestation had set in! He was conspiring to smoke a joint, it was the secret plan! Then Delivering a pizza to Cube (the space center), he's told to go up to the launch pad of the new mine freighter space craft, up to the capsule and hand deliver the pizza to the crew, who then showed him around, he ended up on the second level which was pretty well shut down for launch and dimly lit. the crew which was all females had left him up there going down below to eat their pizza. He knew there'd be no more delivery's tonight! What better way to start the late night, up there downing some of their Bourbon from the cabinet, he got out his sideboar, the Devine Sacred Blessed n Honored Royal Attraction.

0004

JT Jam Toast; 69 Ideal Taste Moods and the Dishes for Mood Dishes!

I   1.   A Highloosingness

2.   Love cloud

3.   Dishes

4.   B What You Will

5.   Tantalizer

6.   .Sugary

7.   Most One

8.   C Operation Mandy Candy

9.   High in Space

10.   D Sight Light

11.   Jam Toast

12.   Resination

13.   E Missing Party at the Party

14.   F Amber Ginger Mellon.

15.   UPHOLDOFF BEHOLDON

16.   Gravy Devotion

17.   Of A Buzz

18.   If A Daze

19   Dazeinger

20.   G Royal Warmth

21.   Kaked

22.   Joint Venture

23.   L.I.P. (lost in place)

24.   H The Smaller Half of Your Universe.

25.   Giving More Massage

26.   I Coco Island

27.   Bow

II   28.   J Inertian Trust Agent

29.   Fantasinaddic Congerationable Jungle Plants Kandyer Stir with Ideal Taste

30. Nectar

31. North East East

32. Star Garden

33. Across the Pond

34. JT

35. Instermentality

36. K. Light Leaf

37. Words without Sound Tell Yourself

38. Pleasure Biscuit

39. L When the Biscuit Wears Off

III 40. M Plume of Smoke

41. Rainbow Shade Shadow

42. Crumb of Intactdecant

43. Kind Kush

44. N Lame

45. Body Machanic

46. Primo

47. O Hippy Lettuce

48. Mixture Element

49. P Know Feel Think See Voice

50. Relish

51. Q Clean Clear

52. Space Wind Earth Fire Water

53. R Cat and the Pussy Cat

IV 54. S Uzona Peach

55. Designed to Jam

56. Sugar Spots

V 57. T Life Love Law Lane Lake

58. Bong Song Gong

60. U Beautyland

61. Energy Shades

62. Inscensations

63. V Detestation

64. Dank Handlin

65 Space Cookie

66. W Lessons in Spacing

67. Getting You Getting Me

68. The Baked Noodle

69th A Leaf in My Tobacco

With Ki's to the Sixth Sensations n Universe*

5:05.9.6.06p-1:30.5.19.17.p

10Y 8M 1W 5D 25m

Summer "86" SC.

10:50.12.26.00p

30¾Y

Main Cast

Ideal Taste; Connoisseur, Mistifist, GSB-(get smart bond), 00786, I.T.A.-(inertian trust agent-Dealer)

Kandyer Stir; Connoisseur, Dutch waiter, (ideals best friend), Dark Diamond;

Soaro; Commander

El D Vapor; 1st officer

Ideal's woman; Uzona Sugarbutter Peach; Sugar Spots, Licky Love

Kandyer's; Sugarcream, Shade Shadow

Soaro's; Sugy Drawer

Vapor's; Honey Love

Puffs

Sept. 6-06

Let's start from a beginning, L.I.P. in Beautyland with lessons in spacing, and I didn't know Munchies Could talk, the Magic Love Life Lane Way! As Craft (the Bands ship) and the three remaining band Members come upon yet another Steller planet, only this one seemed very smokey. Yes the Fueled Monster was intrigued. (the craft ship. We can listen in)

Kandyer;- Our deflectors are weakening we need to send that distress signal!

Soaro;- Hang on!, Vapor light something. I mean it, hang on to something!

Vapor;- We're receiving a response signal from the planet.

Soaro;- What's the planets address Vapor?

Vapor;- Darn map, no address.

Soaro;- What is our situation Kandyer?

Kandyer;- We have crystal depletion, we're caught in an intense cosmic ion storm and we are L.I.P. (lost in place).

RESPONSE;

Female voice;- This is not a coed planet.

Soaro;- I see.

Female voice;- This is the planet Zon, however we have lately been contemplating the acquisition of Husband specimens.

Soaro;- May we float you up on board?

Female voice;- By all means!

Later; You look younger than I expected!

Thank you extremely a lot! I am the leader Honey Love

I am commander Soaro pleased to meet you.

Yes pleased to meet you. As I said we are a planet of from your life scans, how you say women?

And this is Sugarcream and Sugy Drawer.

And it's good to meet you two!

Sugarcream;- And you too all three of ya.

Vapor;- Yes!

Kandyer;- Hi,...Please step over to our scanners ladies.

Sugarcream;- Oh that's out of the question.

Ah just a real Quick one?

Sugy Drawer;- Don't those get a little intiment?

Soaro;-Ah yes, we'll be professional.

Honey Love;- Well OK then.

Vapor;- Sugular!, come ladys.

Vapor;- Commander do you want to see this!

Soaro;- What?

It's Ok ladys, just a little thing with your eyes, looks like you'll all be needing a fresh cup of coffee or Two.

Honey Love;- We must relate to Uzona soon.

Soaro;-Tell me about Uzona!

Sugy Drawer;- She leads us with a keen heat sensitive magnetism, she knows magnetic space hits Without a trace keeping space in its place. She says she's got situations of her own, it's like having a secont you!, "I need your everything and nothing else".

Soaro;- Why don't we all float down, we'll have a party!

Sugarcream;- At Love lake! I don't know if we should keep it a secret, we have a need so great for men! Through her our magnetism is greatly intensified!

What our ladies we're trying to tell them was their predicament they got into when they didn't Compensate certain extra weight and were forced down to the planet and made an emergence Landing from a storm, causing an infection that drove all life on the planet to relocate; Love Idis, It's a minor flesh wound, in the heart! The landing had left Uzona trying to nurse the situation with Ideal Taste high in space with lovecloud dishes lost Joint Venture Jam Toast in Beautyland Bow Relish!

Vapor;- We can't get a fix on the party! Kandyer! Where did they go all the magics gone! Anything?

Kandyer;- Negative! They've been gone for two days! Commander said he'd be back for us that they could save time in smaller groupings. Our primary task is to find corrode Nance located at the party wherever that is?

Vapor;- I've locked onto a corrode Nance though it seems to be jumping in and out of signal Definition.

Kandyer;- Wait a minute those are the commanders molecules bouncing around down there, do you Think he's in some sort of trouble? And where's Sugarcream? She wasn't floating down earlier, then She went to get me coffee, I can't find my coffee either! Open the channel, Thanks Vapor! 1234345 is that you commander?

Soaro;- NOT now! Kandyer give me another hour an a half, two tops, make it two an a quarter Thanks over!

Kandyer;- That's the commander down to a quarter hour, he'll get us down in no time, he's test'in My loyalty,...

...how long we been in radio blackout?

Vapor;- Four hours plus

Kandyer;- To the transporter, work eat sleep play love, the commander baffles me, what's in his Innerspace?...

On Zon

Soaro;- Forgive me you two I must have fall'in asleep, let's have a drink! Sugarcream and Love Honey would like to show you and Vapor around Kandyer, then it's back up to the ship. But first The Divine Blessed and Honored Rich Nug Applicator's Loyal Reaction, it's Royal Attraction, Assist, Aid, Secure, Guard, Track.

Sugy Drawer;- Where are we?

Soaro;- We don't know! All we know and agree on is that this Alien search phenomenon is just a Pet project!

They we're all the saddest ever they we're so happy! Like before the age of the school bus, the Incubus!

Soaro;- Kandyer! I can't account for the ship.

Vapor;- He's having another episode, keep the smoke away; minimize the craving!

Soaro;- She's locked up tight in a scale 10 turbulence! Vapor go bring a supply down! Vapor;- Then just a visit in this. Somebody needs to be on the ship uh once in a while uh! Soaro;- So what's going on Vapor? You're not just going to leave the ship floating again? Vapor;- Dealing in space I know what I face, I need space in a place, see you there!-

This stuff I'm sending you has a luscious fragrance commander - over

Soaro;- It's supposed to be some pretty good- over

Vapor;- I'm not sure the analyzer will handle this kind of quality! Remember Of A Buzz's fried Relay response, resister circuits lost, yea it's always something- over

Soaro;- If we don't check it will we know what to expect? With the price we payed for this Stuff we have to be sure! Is it logical to smoke without analyzation? Logical yes, but it's not human, This is my primary task to believe this stuff, anyway she gave us a pretty good deal!- Can I get a Damage report?

Vapor;-The resin's to much for the screens!

Soaro;- How's the cloud reflector level?

Vapor;- Good! Ship's stable, EI-D-Vapor floating down.

Soaro;- Good I'm out!

It's time for another episode of" On the Side of Your Mind "O.S.M. # 001.007

Come in here foxsexy!

Do you mean it?

I would'nt love you if you were'nt er!... cupcake...pune!

C But I'm going past myself! Let me get orientated, we've got place space, you know the space.

K They've changed their minds

V What, do they know Lessons in spacing? The Tribute, You can' do drugs, so drink alcohol, or, don't Drink an Drive, Smoke an Fly!

Vapor to Soaro the storm has gotten worse, however autopilot is in good working order!

-\El D Vapor for the Kandyer Stir Soaro was Ideal/-

Kandyer;- Sugarcream would ya reload the bongs!? The burn session is inferior!

Vapor;- Get used to it its life! Computers don't lie, although we are still awaiting further Instructions, oh did I mention I jettisoned the Pod! It was just before I was floating down, I Thought she was breaking up, I did'nt know how much more she could take, regulation you

Know. So I stuffed 150 lb's or so of If A Daze er was that kilos? Anyway she's out there somewhere.

Soaro;- Yea our regulation. By the way has anyone checked with regulation today? Vapor;- Fascinating! Sir.

"Ideal walk's in"

Ideal;- Party's over!

Sugy;- Wait we have a confession to make, Ideal's here with us!

Uzona;- I'm Uzona from earth too!

Soaro;- Nice!

Sugarcream;- Yes we brought him.

Uzona;- It was suppost to be a short routine trip!

Soaro;- We were scoping for him when our map went upsidedown, it was three days before we Noticed! By day three we were L.I.P. (lost in place). We would Stumble upon an occasional Weed infested planet, it was miserable until we met up with you ladies.

L.I.P. past 3D, deep into Forebe-4B-Jt at his side. Jam Toast Resination for the missing party nectar East north east, the Plume of Smoke Intactecant, then its Mandy Candy Found in Beautyland, oh here Come's Sugarcream for the T. The Avenue Sight Light Love Drug 4B. Amber-Ginger was coming From the Inertian Trust Agent, his Quest for polishing Hippy Lettuce caked Pleasure Biscuits!

Their journey continued, then continued again, they all found themselves L.I.P. and looking for L.I.P.SA (lost in place satisfaction).

Soaro;- The ship's risking implosion, understand Ideal we've got to risk everything, got to hang on! Never lose never!

Ideal;- We'll thanks that give's me confidence! OK bring her down! Maybe we should check yer Metabolic rate Soaro? (10:51p-12.26.00) 6   (12:08a-11.22.21) 20Y.10M.27D.1H.17m. "Time"

So I'm   fine! That's just the score today! For a moment I thought I was on the bridge L.I.P.G. (going past myself).

So Its clear we have to set up a colony here strait away!

V I agree!

K I'm in favor!

So Right LLLLL (Life Love Law Lane Lake) Ideal!

Uz Go ahead!

I Alright Uzona you know you want it!

Uz I said go ahead!

Sugy Drawer What's your course of action? Your freer in routine Sir.

K Its been rough as traveling singles Miss.

Sugy Sir.

K Sugy Drawer, is this how you behave on your ship?

Sugy Yes!

K Good! We're Pay to Play n Actors!

6418417

Ideal 2nd week First we find the pod!

Acknowledge!

V The ships orbit is similar to the spot the pod was jettisoned. Give me a censer sweep!

Its probably in one of our giant hemp fields!

So We want to thank you ladies for joining us!

You know your #1 on our list to boldly bone where no man has boned us before!

K Well you know we like to space out many new planets, to reack life forms and so on. To the Firm here here, cube!

Ideal I could tell dank handling customs were impressing them with Energy Shades Life Love Law, Wild Turkey?

Ideal you making it?

Ya Kandyer, me an Uzona.

Sugar Spots? Sweet!

Thanks its been sweet, we're in a zone, dank handling customs and all.

Ideal send a communique the nucleolus of our telemetry has dissolved the stars to sky filled fields. A priest might not deduce good reasoning about this thing! Do we have a priest? I don't think we do! Commander we can't pray!

So Are you sure?

Ideal ya we can't pray right, no church! Theres nothing holy about this ship! How can we go on a mission without being blessed? Someone make the sign of the cross.

V If we get up there do you think you can keep it level?

Id That's just it Vapor no one is on the level!

So Ah about that drink you ordered?

Ideal Make it wine, that's what Christians drink, am I right?

Affirmative!

Ideal This is my last entry! It entered well, I'm holding my breath!

V I tell ya there's nota we've gone to far.

Then what's that Kandyer?

Looks like robots, The censors indicate that remote section.

So Vapor, Alert status! Fresh water for the bongs!

Ideal I'm still waiting for analysis over here!

V Right Ideal! It's to far away to get a good reading.

They make it successfully back to the suborbital platform.

Ideal Twist a stick, what'da ya say, fast please!

K Would you wait readout is still printing we don't want contaminated stuff.

V Oh God. We seem to have A malfunction with the analyzer, wait it seems to be arming the destruct sequence! Should we Evacuate!

So If you can't handle it!

V Let me do my job commander, Detonation disarmed!

K Here's the problem commander the T. levels were off the scales, in a good way

Ideal Thanks Kandyer, we'll have to do operation Mandy Candy High in Space! Pass me a Pleasure Biscuit!

The Royal Warmth Caked Joint Venture's; When the biscuit wears off Plume of Smoke! Sugar Cream, Sugy Drawer, Honey Love, is the Missing Party at the Party.

K What's that woman? The mind probing has increased our dexterity and lung capacity!

Agent Sauce

How do you navigate so successfully Soaro? Lately it's been your brownies an sauces Sugy Drawer.

4207410

8:37 2/12/17

Chapter 2

AFTERMATH N ENGLISH

There seems to be some Missing Party at the Party, we think we know where it is, we just Can't get ahold of them and something in the air, that should be, could be, or let's say would be!,

As sensations will hit flow seek from resin nibble beads hanging loosely snagged, their will was getting Low, mind work and body connections at creep'in on the chimney effect!

(Ideal)- Can we get anymore out of her Commander?

(Soaro)- Yea roll one!

(Ideal)- Swirling Spinning Twisting Curling, I might be wing'in it, the derivative is inhibited! Fly'in by in the wink of an eye, he was down being mixed up!

Supplemental: results for- Taste Test- A waste messed, far guessed, less best, the casual toke, The light smoke, it's about a joke! Not exactly Cronic Croke.

After the test (Ideal to Uzona)- "I look at you very well and there's many things I can tell!"

The pod stash was laden with fragrance of Zon, "Daze'inger". Hence Light Daze Space Cron on Of from Zon! A Love Cloud was then finished, soon there was from a Crumb of Intactdecant a Plume Of Smoke forming a second Love Cloud! Kandyer Stirred Nectar's Highlooseingness Kind Kush. Question is are you Munchiaddic? And Polishzing Most One Clean Clear Bow Nectar Instermentality, Or JT's Primo Mixture Element Relish, the Baked Noodle's Fantasinaddic Congerationable Jungle Plants Kandyer Stir with Ideal Taste!, who asking Kandyer, Stir Sight Light Royal Warmth Light Leaf Intactdecant Inscentsation's Gravy Devotion?

Preceiving Dream thought intentions, or Nectar itself, the quality form of JT rarely seen! Last known sighting was the mid 70's. It's Mixture Element Spell Jell effects take over conversing The Telimical Love Drug Noodle Resination done with instermentality in the Cat and the Pussy Cat's East North East Star Garden Across the Pond.

Light Leaf Sight Light Giving More Massage High in Space L.I.P., in a Love Cloud, that gave resination from the Missing Party at the Party!, the Inertian, who had Got'in Lost In Place looking for Nectar somewhere East North East!

Words Tell Yourself When the Biscuit Wears Off the Plume of Smoke of the In-tactdecant is Kind Kush, then it's Lame and were in need of a Body Machanic which resolves to Operation: Mandy Candy. The one for the Cat and the Pussy Cat.

To Beautyland Inscensations Getting You Getting Me the Baked Noodle with a Leaf in My Tobacco. Makes the Hippy Lettuce Element Mixture Know Feel Think See to Relish!, Light Leaf's Primo Luminous Sight, or Party, at Vallyhill High down the way!

Kandyer's look'in for Taste, Soaros the way, Vapor's there.

THC Terpenes Cannabinoids B.S. (Bud Smoke)

HIGH Flavor   Medical 4:48a 9.14.22

9-"86" 10:50p 12.26.00 S:20p 9.6.06 4:20a 6.21.22 Edit- 4:20p-8:45p 9.10.22 / 36Y'

Inertian Trust Agent: Trust to Sugar Bird! Do you have JT over?

Uzona: Yes I'm High in Space, very Clean Clear over!

Inertian: Do you have my bird food! Form from B (Be) form, Polishzing Gravy Devotion JT with The Missing Party at the Party over.

Uzona: Lame its not the same Getting you Getting Me Baked Noodle Joint Venture Body Mechanic Resination, the Noodle Biscuit's Plume of Smoke Kind Kush Nectar! Your covered out-

Love Drugs Clean Clear Words Without Sound Tell Yourself the Smaller Half of Your Universe Know Feel Think See Forebe Giving More Massage!

Soaro: We always seem to get an animal lover on board, I heard someone say someone Burnt their Roach!

The JT and Drug Commander Never Ending Adventures:

Out to the coast Drug commander!

The coast is Clean Clear JT!

She's who we're looking at!

Sugy Drawer? She looks High in Space!

Yes she was resinated earlier this morning!

In real fursure all parcels had reached a new low set for the professionals. Sugar Spots showed Up, it was time for a check with the robots. Things were working out, the stock on the Mineral freighter Just came in handy for the project, and here come the results! Identifying the crisis, the Energy Shades Late with many stresses on their fiber, they were counting on a Mixture Element Kind Kush Relish! Reef sugar was the topic packed away On the Side of the Mind. Energy Shades down the corridor, it was Exploratory. This is the way they think it happened, form was with the breeze, there was a liquid with Flooration, more over there was furthermore! The Weed Need Seed Deed Bead!

Something was missing, a mystery, JT? It was right there On the Side of my Mind. Why was sex So good? Something about Love Drugs? Their power energy specifically generalized, Touch Hearing Sight Thought Feel, this is how Spacing class went. On though the Milky Way Sugy, and they rolled away to Zone Two (couples, Zon) in Craft flavor space futures in you with you within you Love Mate!

It's the first discovery of a habitable planet and its already inhabited by us! Yes Electron Cron Of Zon the newly discovered planet East Northeast in the Star Garden, an Ideal claim! Station Two was A reality, and they rolled away, flavored, in Craft in the Gamma Radiant (solar light extension). Daze'inger 4B was a steep flavor of Electron Cron 4B, not just 3D. With sun planet wind moisture in Time sign season land, not far from the moon with the nug keeper!

Commander this is Sugarcream we have detestations in the area!

Think Partys n nug sugary effectation.

Ideal: Hello, hun open up a jar of honey sugar I'm com'in home, my work is done! Ideal Taste was found! The King Wizard Agent Guardian Hero mellon cron and dawn sugarleaf fly pie herbal essence for Plan C: Sugary space and sugary space music.

1 fox to A fox will you bring me a tray for the tricom crystal cake is done Shade Glade form, To manipulations they know the form for the form. Caused was third Attention packed visions of Meteor hair loss monkeys.

This has been an inside look at the outside, acclamation, additional, wise, knowledge, Understanding smart faith love glory honor, or I did'nt get noth'in, but can you make the next one A little smaller! For the First Attention Impression Dream.

UPHOLDOFF

The August Party

Sex	Thought	Assist
Drugs	Feel	Aid
Rock	Sight	Secure
Roll	Sound	Guard
Party	Speech	Help
Hate	N	Sex
Addiction	E	Ta Tas
Crime	S	Kiss
War	W	Feet
Death	ENE	Seat

What's that group EL an O? I'M a little ofF bAlanCe!, Pink Zap? I don't want to get to close to God, I might bump into him! I thought to him: this is how we talk? He said don't you! To race around, Be in one place going all over and through! From inner outskirts, where wet sunshine is clear black in Gaze haze toxs locs Tranceparent Cell's Sand Pebble Stone Rock Boulder.

I've got to go she says tonight she's not going to Love me anymore today!

Sugar n Honey Bunny Adventures

I.T. Uzona, K Stir Sugarcream

Sugar Bunny, with her best friend giving some sugar honey at the time his friend came, to all go Down the Bunny Hole (specific wormhole) to have T together at the usual spot on Tunea.

Space Time Food, a vision version dream.

And They Happily Lived Ever After

Chapter 3

It was the beginning of their 2nd year. Ideal and Kandyer were focus scoping in nug kake Cutting twilight, when it started an extremely hard rain and within minutes it was darker than a moonless night on earth! Kandyer saw the flash light beam and yelled Ideal! The beam was coming his way again then he yelled no but it was gone. Dashing ahead right into a tree branch, wondering where approximately forward went, these rains went on for days quite often, soon they were each LI.P.

After initiation, a tribe the Fuwtrotions (there are not many serious mistakes in this tribe) Treated Kandyers wound and he was again feeling fine!

Meanwhile Ideal had gotten into the stock where he had been elected to run a village he Came across, the Gowbess known for their quality smoke! And he was caught by a watchman and Knocked out. Making his way to a local Dr. he was feeling fine!

The Morals to the stories are fabled!

They needed congroupulation. And Kiff Trycoms (the investigator sent by Cube to secretly Check conditions and life on Zon when first discovered) was he at the Gravyation with Zonacron?

Some days of eventually! With you with me to top the subliminal mind, Dramatica Dramatico Sugar Spots, Ideal was back looking into her eyes reminded of his impression when he first saw her at the hatch "Where have I been all my life"

They had made it back to real civilization.

Ideal: Sugar Spots will someone please find Inspector Trycoms and tell him again Honey Love Is look'in...look'in for him?

Soaro: Air Waters Earth and fire if we only had that stuff on this planet!

Vapor: What's this stuff anyway?

Soaro: sure I'm gonn'a tell you again!

Vapor: I like the drugs with vitamins an minerals! Trycoms went away.

Soaro: Fabway

Vapor: Yes Dataway! Taste is around, I think he's using Technology Astrology

Chemistry Science and Biology, he will find him.

The party was Too Good to be Bad, preform and you get performance!

Coming soon "ENERGY SHADES'= Heaven, Hell, and possibly the Land of Space.

Diamonds	Plastic	Courage	Time data
Emerald	Iron	Bravery	Bulk data
Safire	Wood	Truthful	Volume data
Ruby	Rubber	Unselfish	Liquid data
Pearl	Glass	Loveable	Temperature data

The Land of Space

The King, Trycoms, Pizza, the Cravers! They had built the castle spending their time seeing, there Were delivery's to be made. Star Angle (Uzona) was always there. In the gamma Radiant (Astrology's) Time marks for the clock of earth. Milky Way configuations etc.

Solid what we need are Enabler Reeferance shifts! For one of the Lords might, even the king or two! Space Wind Earth Fire Water's Wheat Corn Bean Rice Potato! After dinner it was a L.I.D. (lost in a Dilemma), taking LSB, listed Stats of A-Drug to B-Cell-ratio, apparently there are two kinds A and B. and the Dream Conscious Subconscious Subliminal Mind, Visions Telekinesis Telepathy ESP Mind Control Transference Trip.

Coming to the future, the Alien Beast Stew n Brew, serving Redbrowner-gold76 (hash oil).

As Zaz City dusk moves slowly over the Horizon

The Galaxy was getting a Royal Warmth, the King and Queen from earth were making a visit To Sugar Dish Castle. They prepared even though they were Lost n Spaced.

Ideal: Got it! Shall we light the way?

Kandyer: Will I go through something?

Ideal: Through it and beyond! It'll pass, will it register? Fresh inscentsations and new Lessons in Spacing, primo hu? All that rolling away to Station Two!

Consumed by a cloud, cloud consuming consumers that are just a consumption. It's the last Night of Aug, it's time for Realyation! My woman is more magnetic than a Black Hole! Don't you need To check the rocket fuel in a rocket somewhere, sometime right away?

Makinitinspace

Bounce time was miss calculated. Your off course, better check with... What a new flight plan? Landing patterns?, to Tany town!, in bush mountains, you can usually find the mountains, but Tany town! Its somewhere near Micro city? Up there these alien beasts get the Love sugardolls and corner them, the Love sugardolls are so frightened, if no one comes along the girls can starve! The Jgeaks! An Urp! Availmonuals! All of them you know.

Ha haw!

Hay thanks, no one came along, I'm starving.

We'll on to opening night at the Groove n Flow, were on level two in the Pink Peach!

For the Action Adventure Mystery Horror Love Thriller Spy Drama!

Hope you are enjoyed!

(if you haven't truthfully enjoyed! You'll be wanted in manipulations)

Castles built around a van?

They don't know!

Pizza van ua? He used to live in a van!

A continued Adventurism

Lum'in Loft Lumber Zat.

Hi are you from Cube?

Yes Cube: here to take you as far as you want to go!

Name's Minky can I help you?

Let's go outside!

Light what end?...This looks like the end!

Ideal Taste will be back in Ideal Space! For the cause? I'm for the effect! He's a Sugar Bird: A rare breed. You might say very mate oriented, though the male often rarely fly's down to the Pond (the Pond: local bar two poles down from the light) for drinks with the boys! Very sharing birds often eating Each other's food!

(Brought through with youto buy Earth Fire Water Factories and soon the Air Factory!)

Genetic Boarder to physical Center

Thought Fantasy Vision Dram OBE (out of body experience) and the Space Wind Earth Fire and Water to have see are do~be in Place Base Space Taste Lase. A review by- THE INTERSTELLER TELLER - We request some of your Undivided attention!

By Sherlockwatt

Kandyer! What do you think?

It's almost like what happened almost! He (Ideal) was crimular, he reeked of inascentury, he followed the basic model rule: Use yourself so that you may use others! He's been looking On the Side of his Mind, often visiting the Alien Zoo, constantly commenting on the intriguing sign out front, "Please Don't Eat the Animals! And that the cars on Zon move like Halys comet with the Man in the Moon Driving!

Reporting for the future of the future.

Beholdon

Dec. Party

Terror Cart Mobbing Thief Ganging

Big Foot	Wizard	Expansion
Yeti	Elf	Addition
Abominable Snow Man	Fairy	Increased
Sasquatch	Hobbit	Fed
Boogey Man	Lepricon	Lifted

Netherland	Weed Dragon
Israel	Flying Fish
America	Sea Horse
Britain	Dolphin
Australia	Stingray

Formula

1	2
Mushrooms	Iowaska
San Pedro	Datura
Ergot -related	Bella Donna - related
Marijuana	Salvia
Iboga	Papaver (Poppies)

10:52 p 12.26.00 4:42 p 6.3.22

21Y 5M 1W 16H 50m

Chapter 4

Cube teck- I know what I think I do, ua we seem to have lost place of the planet, we know Delima-C section scanned but we can't place exactly where it was from? You see we are responding To a very small microbial like area, very small, ran by a computer with more feeling than a human!

Ion

Electron

Neutron

Proton

Kake on

Supplemental: (Ideal Uzona)

She said treat me right! I said you don't want to be left? Swarmed by smoke in a kind of a smoke Swarm. I said I want to see you in my morning!

This Subquardrant ENE Gamma Radiant of the Milky way.

At the Casual Extravaganza

The discovery of Zon had led to other habitable planets. Here's an article we've intercepted From the planet Tuna an article on Zon, in Lover Girl mag., named Y is Who Where and When? An Ad Really advertising the planet: Cigarette for a Cup of Coffee? A position and place where you can relax and take it easy at the same time! Leaving Deep Edges.

Unknown source: the diversity central of their species was so diversifiable. I thought of it actually an conciteral averigistic part, not so? We here believe being contemporary would end this.

Back in the day one day,

Do you have a name?

No sir, do I Sarg.?

Another thing I heard, on the King an Queen's flight, Zim and Zpock we're at the helm, Zones however, was with the alien creature, an alien taking human form in the appearance of a woman Who looked like she didn't drink or smoke but does. The creature, about to spike his drink when a call Came in on his communicator someone had been hurt on the deck below, someone the alien had rendered helpless in; phase one, incapacitate Zones: He turned only to catch her-it-the-thing! In the act! Still in female form, Zones easily subdued her-Carrie-the thing!

Ops got to go, Baked Noodles with Rye.

Mutiny for the Bounty; -Love kake

Tuneataters, the heads of a civilization far in the distance! Their Replicanics and associlale resiellized Particle? Pass, Just kidd'in I'll play, what's a score? What!

This has been a five beer mission in the Place Shuttle.

Dragon   Leach   Spider   Snake   Rat

1 Fox to A fox; come in, over-

I'll be over, over-

Bring the Sugared Electricer, over-

L.I.T. Association

(lost in thought)

Check out that #1Being hit song; "YA MAKE ME MAD'

I suppose you are wondering who's coming in when? The woman above! Not Precisely Percistion with The submorpher smoothly cornered true; around to where he was going through.

We'd like to thank SUGAR BISCUITS made by Sugared Pasture, for sponcering.

Another coffee cigarette?

Above Perfect

Below Perfect

In between Perfect

I think I remember I mistakenly picked B, Perfection Below, it was D all the above!

Once the Grand High Master had read this far he paused, sending a fax that read, "Well Done Grasscricket!"

A Mystery Van Importion.

Rama   Park   Fair   Circus   Carnival

Get I T, Ideal Taste

See ya at the Burn Garden.

Text Sir. A Free B

(Ideal): I consider myself High as I have to look down upon the Earth, or, or is that Tunea? How long has the map been upside down!?

In theaters this spring the Creepy Horrifying "Less Lights"

Few words in this story were Mistreated, Harmed, or even Misspelled and Upsideumop!

Funded by NSF Global White Widow Blueberry, Pineapple Cheese. (NICE SWEET FINE)

Did Craft meet up with a stolen mine freighter- these stories and more on Deductive News

All of a sudden I'm getting no life readings on the Ultraprize!

Sorry, plug it back in again, I tripped on the cord.

Sun Cloud Dark Shade Light, he would always ask that question (Ideal): Do Ya Like me with Love?

Apithetic Apathy

REALYFECTION

Dissipation

Ideal: I need Hawaiian Bubblegum, I'm coming down with Strawberry Cough

Uzona: Stop at D Pizza!

Ideal: Hello I would like to order a flavored Future Werknhappen Firm pizza, watch the gears babe don't shift us out of pepperoni, onion, mushroom, olive n Zon bacon unadominal we're still traveling at 155,000 Miles an hour.

To the Love Limb Festival

Further Footage

Here with Mood Dish Nectar Reiish Gravy Devotion, at the Love Limb Festival for ship arrivals from Zon, coming in soon, this will be filmed in Rousing Action, with just sparing no expense but a little, often.

Nug to Zuhookua do you copy?

I am reading you.

Nug. Kandyers middle name.

12009706A

20031610A

Hows Soaro Kandyer?

Cherry map!

Vapors blown away, so we can't get D positioning.

Sugy Drawer D map!

See GSB gets on up to the barracken!

Right sir. There's a major storm com'in, can I barrow yer laser?

Sill smok'in?

Cosmosive

The mission with the Tuneataters not far behind: Z10 has had a complication: Contained Static, it's the best, called project Rainbow Candy, causing a slight rein grain, its cosmosive!

Ideal: Sugarm aid Fox let us know Zab will be at the festival, they will attempt to mix Tiger Kake And Amber Gingermellon for Ginger Tiger Kake Amber. Grab a Dish Biscuit for the Beholdon (Dec. Party) Dezined to Jam!

OSM Episode 769.786 Operation: Snake Kake.

Bet?

Bet Dr.! Give me a min. This end?

You get your snack!

D Pizza?

Get me the Light Gam gun, the first aids and the Gravity Bong for them and the mission

White Wolf cub

Falcon

White Horse

Rapture

Eagle

Instinct Astounding

Rudiralus

Thai Stick* / Strawberrycough* - Moonrock* / Bow* / Skunk* / Columbian Gold* / Columbian Red Bud*

Phantom cookie	Aquapuco Gold*	Astronaut Bud*
Chronic*_ Strawberry Cheesecake*	Kana Gold*__Cookie OG	Green Shock
Hawaii Maui Waui*	Gold Thai*	Gorilla Cookies
Blue Dream*	Kind Lime	Bubble gum*
Hash Plant__Color of Space dles	Blueberry*__ Zai Zai	Forbidden Zkid-Bx2
Tangerine Dream*	Panama Red*	Cherry Bomb
Wookie Cookie	Royal Purple Afghani*	Cali Orange
Banana Split	Mexican Rainbow Trip*	Head Cake
Green Love Potion	Coco*	Sugar Breath
Space Candy	Lambsbreath*	Peyote Cookies
Cotton Candy press*	Crystal Bubblegum	Pineapple Ex-
Jilly Bean	Mouchuawahcon *	Sweet Tooth
Blue Bubbler Yum*	Black Sheba*	Fat Banana
Nebula	Blind Sight	B C God Bud
Texada Time-Warp	Love Fight	Gods Treat
Christmas tree bud*	Wrong Right	Jelly Rancher
Gainesvill Green*	Heavy Light	Gorilla Girl*
Gorilla Glue*	Day Night	Grape Ape*
Girl Scout Cookies *	All about a few things	Lemon Tree*
Cream Sizzle	Valued J 48 T Formula Magic	Vietnamese*
Cookie Glue	Deserts Swirl Earth	Purple Candy Cane

TYE WILDNCOOL

*Red Hash**		*Waters Whirl*	*Water*	*Peanut Butter Breath*
*Blonde Lebanese Hash**		*Trade Wind Twirls*	*Air*	*Catatonic Hash Oil*
*Garfield OG**		*The Neural*	*Space*	*Hash Oil**
*Gorilla OG**		*Unfurl*	*Fire*	*ICC* {Ice Cream Cake)*

4:20a 6.21.2022 from 10:50p 12.26.2000   21Y. SM. 3W. 40. 5-1/2H. T.W. Time

Chapter 5

On Down to Earth

This is no BS (band in space), so we are BS (behind the scene), actors waiting here at the JBL Building (just drug love}, awaiting the arrival of other ships on earth. We brought back a bit of the Zan coffee, it's more like a pinyon seed, better to eat it, almost. Oh here's Owand (tunea ship), their a bit off course. Oh! their taking out a chunk of that west field, every body grab a baggy!

Med Pep Man seemed to be there singing, it Legendarily goes:

I.T., Uzona, K. Stir, Sugarcream:

"In the distance gone with one bong, 00769 went down Moore Pass Span, tak'in a Token Scope In the Burn Garden near Vallyhill at Tany town at the Gravyation, there he met Dark Diamond about THCBS and the Zesty report. They later met Shade Shadow and another female (Licky Love) at the Brunch n Munch to get KSSST!

Hav'in just returned from the Festival please check one:

-Pretty Good

-Very Fine

-Exaddicly Phunomenic

-Hav'nt Lit Up?

Sample Twist.

Shade Shadow, she helps along, owns a gong, and a bong, she says things go up; and things go down,. when they really just hover round. She had found microscopic life was fine too. She should be reporting in. Some say she knew Uzona?

This is Soaro to the Ultraprize do you copy?

This is the Royal Nodual!

Sorry!

Reformulating the formula

Vacationing Eruptions Zat, what really happened?

The phycodelic Jams with Sugary Spices will be at the SDC (sugar dish coin) show. A beyond Sun and Moon gift Treat! Chocolate Chip?

-N-

Static-charged Effort-missma (miss or manage) Attain-sustain Afford-applctic

This has been the everending beginning for when the mountain clouds come down home. Thanks to;

Miguel

112013010P

Myusht Mellon Ltd.

Hidden Secret page Mystery

We left waiting for Wampuma as she finds they have Licky Love from Croke Toke Smoke Choke Soak in the air. She knew they were there. She knew she had'nt smelled the aphrodisiac fresh cut smells since last time GSB was in. She missed it, him! And there's those edible scents again, tantalizing, she had! Been to collage. 4:07 7.14.17p addition

The first thing to do was contact Dr. Lovebones about Glass ice, which is where both sides fill in, a Mysidebrains condition, calling for Dalisha bud!

Virtually no vulnerability, so by injecting funds that way, excuse me… Hello…yes hun… sure it exceeds Dividens, what did I say? Get them in the Gopper Stopper and when their not look'in that's when you Really let them have it, ua I'll have to go. No vulnerability leading to Snug Observation.

Memo; QB stated the ZX7 disappeared, GSB?

Wake n Bake

Emerald Edge Crystal Quarts Stone Zat Man!

-I will Read for you-

A man comes, he travels fast.

He brings violence.

Hum He has purpose

Doesn't sound like 00786

Above Loves

You knew the answer, strangely so will I!

Taste the Cookie

I didn't know yer still here. I Just got here, yes I was sitt'in wonder'n where I was at when I noticed I was here!

El Dopeo

Live n Fly

Licky Love

She was the kinda spy she was! If I know what I mean?

Mission of Mysidebrains Miss Wampuma, update me.

N you startled me, well00169;the triplets and GSB are contacting Licky Love. I'll check with SPYC Manipulations n Z5n get back to ya.

Faith, or what we like to call smarts of the future, is how we like it here at Peppermint Pepper Pipes n papers etc.

55012310A

Here's ta 2012 see ya on the other side

It was the summer house summer. Mysidebrains Germinator, the alien terrifyer, we hope to find our hope. This secret weapon horrifyer, its germinate deep into the edge of the woods to the deeper dark Forest.

All I could think about was cupcake, when she said you'll have to go through our scanners also! And We'll be discreet too!

There's her voice! I see her moving over there at the side of the room. I just noticed. She's probably Been there the whole time! All of these years I've been sitting here? I'll have to stop writing to see what She wants, apparently she's been? Sponging me! To the Primo Royal Warmth! In the side of your mind Buzzo. Will the Intactdecant T avenue open If A Daze Dank Handl'in Space Air Earth Fire Water Highloosingness Nectar High in Space Resination Kind Kush Relish.

Bring in the Royal Croke Toke Smoke Choke Soak Redbrownergold with its backgammon complexity. Rolling space futures Zat, cylinder zone, shaped for your involvement arid borrowed for Space Sports Uncalculated!

With the same different coin co. promise, the same of the same!

11212110P

Top Secret

-only photo, suspected to be "Castle", received by agent, the Triplets we're a big help, I mean that singularly. The Cloaking device was temperarely disabled due to snow like storm.

There seems to be a thing, I'll stop here at Love Bone Beach on the pipe sea!

3-6-7:57-20

5:55 4.3.20

1:12

TRUMPLAMENTAL

Clean Clear Mixture Element Magnetism Designed to Jam with Gravy Devotion Of a Buzz, L>I>P> Jam Toast Polishzing! Kakey need a lighter, yer the lighter ok? An the Kakey Stony Stoners Strawberry Tea {KSSST), to have Carmel Fruity Ginger Cinnamon Blueberry Kiwi Cherry down at Coco studios.

OSM Episode 101.017

BUSH FLOWER

Your so hot a spatula...

Mere, I mean Doc.

Meet me in my office!

Patient 137 Doctor!

Not 137, I thought he's off studying at medical school?

He is studying something at that school, I think that's why he needs us!

It's the medical marijuana thing again isn't it nurse Foxsexy?

Why Who What When Where

With 000's Woman on mission infezable*

About Operation DROP BACK O-girl! I remember that tight spot: Wake up we're about to be busy! N made possible the papers that convincingly, starring us: diversion, with the Triplets, Bong Song and Gong, will Agenotics Delecasys Class would have said, Primo Elements Biscuits answer?- Maybe. Then when you got back it was "She's been through a hole jar of coffee" we're goin'a check her out! (nurse)- I suggest a breather in the garden woods Doc._]

It appears to be the Royal Nodual ship, get the sugar leaf ready! We need to phase the field. The phasers didn't phase it. Phase out the phasers! It's alright one pass works, its very very tough stuff. On the level, what's on the level? These we're the bar trips of the Ultraprize. Done with thunder Wonder pictures. & My Hearts Broken in Records.

To Moor Pass Span to phase the field, remember you'll need some reduction in the inducer; Zuhuca.

Their not responding Capt. Wait, left behind, sinking slow, way far to go. Yes their L.I.P.Z. (lost in place zoncrainics).

Call for James Franks, James Carmalborne Franks!

Bonus song footage

-U-

U UUU U UU U U U U U

UUUUUUUUUUUUUUU

UUUUUUUUUUU

UUUUUUUUUI

(SUNG AS IF YOU MEAN IT)

-To Get Her That

Barbequed Fish

D tonight Special

To get her there that you must first contact another world.

Another world please hold. Another world, what's that? You wish to make contact? I think you want another dimension!

Another dimension, can I help you?

I wanted another world!

Please hold.

This is the 54th 80th dimension go ahead with your order, our special is Barbequed Fish!

Have A Nice Night

Dear; To on Earth. Where Chip players stick on continue, and the Amber Ginger Mellon in the garage joint.

Bowk Soap

OSM Episode-086.007

Nurse can you figure this out?

Let me see, you'll have to break it upa little more Doctor. Try some Hash Doc.

Extreme Complete your check an dose him, we've got thing to do, I'll be in my office!

N.

Wampuma.

We have a message from Z5- from ruler Zab- D pizza was above decent. King and Queen have left

With your Love Leaf Soap

Jemgold n Sugarmaid Fox in

Tiger Kake Burnish

What is it babe?

I'll need ya to make Kake!

Also starring Zcotty, back from a brief major set back, capt. The Warp engines their Worped!

Fur Fox Make Conjuror Revel Work Have

24010209

Approx.42010209a

Extra Paper

OSM Episode- 007.007 Double Dube

Nurse you'll have to roll one!

But I never!

I know something about it Doc.

Nurse.

But I don't know if I can roll another one just yet, give me a min. I'm like when trying to spell a word, only having myself to turn to, I don't know what to tell my-self; I thought you didn't know already? Its like when nothings been said and ya sill take it the wrong way.

Play Work Live Survive Exist

Track Dream Scout See Feel

Complements of the Pink Peach's Smell Roach Café

Space, and that Final Beer, and she's like mak'in Barbie look like a doll!

Thanks;

OLDER YOUNG

MINCE SAME DIFFERENT COIN CO.

RENDERING

PICKLED PEPPER BRUNCH N MUNCH

GARDEN EATERS

MOONSTONE INC.

PLUM PEAR PEACH CHERRY LEMON

BS; BAND IN SPACE, BEHIND THE SCENES

PLUME OF SMOKE - POND BAR

BAKED NOODLE

ALIEN BEAST STEW N BREW

EASTWING

GROOVE N FLOW

PINK PEACH

BLEND BEER

INTERSTELLER TELLER

ALIEN ZOO

LOVER GIRL MAG.

L.I.T. ASSOCIATION

SUGARED PASTURE

MEMBER OF THE WEEK AFTER SUNDAY

SPICIFIC GENERAL

THAT MAG.

FABERJ RADIO N TELEVISION

CRITTER CRISPS

Chapter 6

M.O.P.

Posh Heat Friction Time Perticularance! Today there is a low followed closely by a distant wind! It's just the Earth Gene, Magnetic Globular Reaction, Dissidences of the Glob! God Christ, scene Clause Gravity, leadership Safety Custom Brave Clean.

Get the Sustain Dept., we've heard from GSB, the Power Sight section, who said, he's had a problem with ESB, whoever it is won't quit thinking about him! (extra scensery bombardment) Let me give you a quick peek at my theoryology, when he said Mental Hygiene! I knew what he meant, expressive Reflextic. "I was look'in for the mountain taste and got the valley". He picked himself up, and a few things, he's back!

Note of FABERJ: Who's Modal Moto Memo: You are you, is you!

Tell him to Get Smart the Missions Impossible!

Touch Eat See Be Breathe

THIS tALE IS Bean ModiFIED tO bE ORiginAL

Tok'in Space Toke you really need Space to Toke. Doobie Do Do Do, Hungery? May I Suggest Condensation or I have these Critter Crisps, made with real Alien Life Forms! And packed With Protein Microbes!

Extended Version

Sugar control: Having Picture Word Lights God Savior Saint Prophet, Ideal; I was at the bottom Of Heaven, feeling the force of the power and the beauty that Widens the eyes. A Considerable Amount of Zonians might Consider that Considerate Considering? It's far ahead in our story, Pro Ace Master (any one of the Band) checked n scoped Dull Ditchable Clip Fed Light Echos, like a condensation.

Done for the Engrossed income

Daze corp.: It helps to do the extremely impossible for the extra power! Remember space for That final Beer! It was time for Calmity, anything else? Oh! that kid's question, the of why does the moon Just hang up there in space? Simple I allow it to.

Note: Play the B side of YA MAKE ME MAD- I THINK I WANT TO KISS YOUR TONGUE!

One day down at the Coulderwould shop, Deboto and a CR Modulant 5 spoke in passing: Deboto: I'm programed for a dozen languages!

CR 5: I have more than 50 primary functions, and the finest hallucinatory glands, the 180 Q Tip Touch! Funny

Ideal: Tunea sure was a pretty sight wasn't it?

ITA was wondering about the inspector? The Queen of Sugardish had become a delicately Sensed balance. GSB's last message ended with" I'm gonn'a get a good days sleep! What Did he mean Daze? He has been reported Missing Lost. At about the same time the Subcar disappeared along with the Zesty Papers, a report on a project with a prolific way of turning things on and off. He also said "Remember Minus Divided Times Plus. SPYC out.

BOWNESS PAGE PART

A Poem Bye

Perfect

Is Perfect

Just Perfect

Perfect Enough

On a Cloud in a Cloud

Toltec

Back to wrong News, and in the wrong news tonight; something seemed to go wrong with the. Electrical equipment in the warehouse that caught fire yesterday?

Was it wrong when in agenotics Jr. year class, GSB's assignment was "the Fiend was about to light up his mission stop him at all costs".

GSB on that toughest hard mission. She was suppose to tell you I got mad and left! She should of Told you I went Mad, left Mad! I will always have a cigarette with my Martini. So I go Mad, got to smoke in the streets ya know!

How pervasive of you to be so perceptive, pretty persuasive. He went out the side of his mind! He was really outside of his mind!

42040109A

Easter

Try n Remember what Frick Enreal would say, Steep Deeply Above, there's only so much we can do, so we'll do more!

He'll get to the Bottom of it, even if he has to go High!   42042609P

The Tracking Dreaming and Intent

Being-Substance-Attribute Accident-Essence-Necessity-Intellect

Dish Kake! Is GSB here!

Zoombuggys still gone!

Assist Help Prevail View Place, and then get out of here!

QB said be sure to remember to burn.

A Coco Californic Tai Afghan Amster Rainbow Red+

Before the age of the school bus the Incubus! They we're all the saddest ever they we're so happy!

Insane   Sickness Crime   Murder Injustice

Member of the week after Sunday group.

//CUT//

Check for Flower buildup!

OSM Episode- 001.0099

Intermixed Focus Factor Force

Your not in there smok'in?

No! I'm not, why Miss Pusskitten, I'm getting you some pills.

Cause if you are I'm swallow'in this key!

Cough!

Gam gun! Get Group two: And the gravity bong for them and the mission:

Octopus

Blue Jay

Sea Turtle

Lizard

Carnal

Maybe a mind jel for strength weakness.

The mission with Furtherness, the Tuneataters not far behind.

Z10 called the ZX7 just arrived, it's Dark Diamond, looks like Fantasinaddic Congerationable Jungle Plants with Ideal Taste with Zesty Papers for Zesty Paper stuff: Exeactexact, Nytrare.

Sex	Drug	Jewel	Money	Love
5Do	4Control	3Grab	2Enjoy	1Have

Memo: For GSB- Chemicalphysics class: at 11:15 Hum...finally...hotties.

Cloverberry SMOKED FRUIT

D Outer Space Pizza Place

Here's a side angle view from BS (behind the scene's) It's the Rocket bringing the Castle to Earth relocating it at the Original Puzzle Bone Beach on the Pipe Sea. With Lobster Pizza Steak Lamb Pheasant!

/HOGLEG/

-Son of the Man with the Golden Gun-

GSB, Uzona: I thought the Mission was going for routine when intensity intregacy was a buffer Integrity, then, she won't but she does, n she will but she don't, steps in.

I Ganga go, Ruderalus!

You

Should

Be

Kind

To

Other

Aliens

Formula=4BC

One- B- 3D_ 4B- 5= 4C

Sweet Potato Syndrome

You'll notice this one when you become so engrossed in reading, you find your barking off Order after order, yea, get me that, an see if the extra lighter is there, I might need I.T., Further an Farther, then finally you make a little space, cause she's been standing there with more than two things In her hands when you realize you need a drink!

The Space Place Case Lase Ace

Fureal Fursure

MENU

D's Cool n Wild Buff n Fluff Tuff in Stuff;

Aged Enriched Protenincive

Patty's for the Past, Present,

Future, Future of the Future

And Beyond!

Try The

Assorted Field Variety

Original

Mountain Hoppers

Or Fly Candy

New

In the coin fields

With the Gem plants

Buff one off tonight!

With Actors n actresses, Producers n Directors?

Cheech n Chong, Goldie Hawn

Chevy Chase, Kurt Russell n Bill Murray

Agent Detective Inspector Mcnoodle Burn-n-Puff

Stash Page

To the Aug. 1st Upholdoff and the Dec. 1st Beholden.

I hang out in Space, I.T.'s a real Place.

Choice casting: Raelynn

Brittany Murphy

Shirly Eaton

Jody Foster

Amy Smart

Anne Farris

Kimberly Williams-Paisley

Mandy Baxter

Brooke Shields

Carrie Fisher

Lacy Chabert

Kaley Cuoco

 Smokers Section

Reminder- Eat your Pizza from the Fish place, Calamari-

Do Go Be See Clear

Cool Plaz Ray Mag Smudge

Formula usages:

1. Gam gun

2. Tool

3. Neckless

4. Lock

5. Flyer

6. 5th Element

7. Discovery

8. Flight Machine

The SUGARPRIZE

In the distance, you could hear the concert.

Chapter 7

Span

Action Nick Burn

in

GRIP VISION

So yer by yourself, so I'll come over and be by yourself too. (Will Regeneration)

Take the Acquasition pill for Mysidebrains.

Tak'in to D Pizza Licky Loves Sugar Noodle was in mysidebrain Germination to avoid it we called her Licky Lov Noodle and pressed on to the New Jam Toast, Dank Handie'in Relish Nectar all the way.

The Tuneataters want to check about Pod stash. Lets look in on GSB's Live BS action (behind the Scenes) as he try's to alert them! As he starts talking to them he try's to tell them the Tuneaters Haven't gott'n a sample, I believe they called it Yum Gum!

They went off to work on the latest project, making Ginger Tiger Mellon Daz'nger Zon Cron or Crystal Bubbleyum.

ZS says inspector Trycoms is meeting with the Tuneataters then with Nick, I guess their also look'in For the Inertian Trust agent.

Ideal your Nick! Just a Connusseur, Kandyer, that's the way I roll! Back at the Party, which lasts a Month, Sugy Drawer, Love Honey, and Kaky we're at the Castle when someone came though the wall. Kaky need a lighter, yer the lighter! The Dalisha bud is curing our condition, them tuneataters! Let's Head to the Alien Beast Stew n Brew El Dopeo. Right bring the Pinebutterapplescotch for the Smelly Roach! Munchy Man.

OSM Episode 123.321

Beginning End

Here's my picture.

You were cute when you were young!

What?

We'll then you grew up.

What?

Cute!

M.O,P.

Movie on Paper

The High Joint

The Day Aftermath

Ideal

Kandyer

Why aren't you burning that/

Sugar Cup n me are gonn'a do Resin Lick detail. The spray Cleaner. I was caught smok'in in the JDL building bathroom again! Bummer. What's this?

Crystal Bubbleyum! Get the Chillum

Cough- Its aliens honey their after me.

Eaze off baby their after me too

You two ain't right, but you are!

Help me make it through the light!

10 Years in the Baking

Gone in the Wind

Another story by Tai

Nice Space n Place far far away. There's about to be a real Spyc Deal.

Hun you and this smoke are better than a dream, Reality.

Let's go eat some cactus!

Better order a Barbeque Fish pizza.

There's aliens of another race in our place and database, smok'in!

Yes dear things grow together.

Edit; 9:17~'7*21A17*

It's time for OSM.

OSM Episode 007.690

In Future Stones

Yes your beautifulness, we can get the best, ok we'll get the rest.

Hello give me everything you got!

I was right in the middle of someone!

Sssss We are having technical difficulties beyond our control, we will return you to regular Predetermined functions thank you.

Pass me the marmalade wine Kake Kat.

Sssss

That's right leafless tobacco, I know it can't be done, can you do it? Not only will they make you see colors but you can touch em too!

Sssss

Do you have any Girl Scout Cookies?

I saw them with the Death star and the Butterscotch Cinnamon Vanilla Carmel

Sssss We now rezoom are regularly scheduled program already in progress.

The Boldly Beautiful

You think I don't think, you think, you know I'm about 3 days ahead of my time! Is Tommy getting Out of jail in time to get his sister when she's released from the hospital so they can make the mortgage payment by tonight's deadline? I don't think!

Soon to come, Puss n Booty a Wild new book!

In the future "stones" another new book.

The Stop Page

Time to Toke watch the Tele in Black n white n colors and listen to the distant-mine freighter launch

With striate from the back room, Sugar Puff, the Stuff

Goodnightime love zesty, Roll.

Roll one?

That too,

Again ok!

5259606

5259916a

Glossy

Sweetspicy; Enterjaytour the pie and video parts of the mind where mysidebrains are. Pronounced International Intergrator Interjator Interjector. Too much pressure causes noodle sandwiches. We hope you've been activated by the pretencive content.

Major J. to Buzz Cat

Yes Taste and Stir are into another mighty mission code named; Puff, Ideal's middle name

Stop by the Perky Pepper for Sonic coffee.

This was Ideal to Taste.

Edited   125921817a

45431017-version p

THE END

Summer "86" SC a Beginning

Summer of "86" SC still morning, beatin the breakfast menu change, in the dinner across the highway from the hotel with the band, Treg is being born! Mr. Auro never made it to paper.

Began Ideal Taste	10:47 12.26.00p
In-Genius writing Starts	5:00 9.6.06p
Finishes	Appox.4:20 9;9.16p
10Y.2D.23H.20m	

I couldn't see it but it could see me, then Light n Dark n Flickr n Spark on a plane from somewhere Else, Alien germinator terrifier or Love in a box.

The Given Taker was here

Independence day 4th of July RASANA version.

Mental Physical Emotional Sight Sound 4:20?8.5.2017

Edit n pre Regg 4:20 Pineapple Breath Taker p. 7.7.17

Sugar Dish (SDC) - Out ... (Often known as The Alien Love Castle)

Written In-Genius...

Twenty Tiny Trailing Smoke Rings from my Chillums end 4:20-7.14.17p

Dis Appearing with David Copperfield the 14th time

-Non Medical and above 5:00p 7-17-17 print-

And *7:01*7*21*2017/10:27*7*21*17*p. Edit 7:14*8.4.17pm Art included, Gorilla n Pineapple Mixy 00769.

1st Annual Space Truck Space Race

Bird Butter Inc. Bud n Flower Race 2.000.000·

Biting bites into the cleavage* of turn one! In the lead, the worm. (Aeronautical term)*, last place Winged Winggo. 6:15.5.5.18p

10:50.12.26.00p 17Y 4M SD 19.H 35mm

Wrap up page

Giv'in Dream like powers Biting Worm's driver was still seeing stars as he approached the Atmosphere in the lead on the last lap of the space race, winning the first annual Space Truck Space Race with flying colors all around!

Race fans can view the B. Worm at the sponsors website.

www. D Midnight Lunch Menu Blend Beer@Stutter Licious blot kom

Remember to catch the premiere of the B.S. of the Mind. (back side)

2:08a12.20.17from10:50p12.26.00

Tai Wildncool

Raizon granules were almost permanently depleted they were so low, but he would fly in upsidedown if he had to, he'd been in the lead the last half of the day!

2nd n 3rd place we're through the atmosphere too. (Intensly Tensive n Glazed Dislove)

Wrapped

Againgg   Gluy Ouwy Guwy

OSM

Episode- 000.018

THE CONDENSER

Pipe 5

A little smoke#3

T7 lighter

Preparer to Prep

But first let's condense!

Hollywood's phone's ring'in it could be the Party at Palm Beach' West Palm Beach's place ring'in, For the answer machine's song intoxication, maybe talk about NYC.

Guwy Gluy Ouwy GG again

Have departed for the Mossy Mushroom-

Bow Wow...

4:55.1.4.18p from 5:20.9.6.06p

THE END

Last day on Zon zoned out n about, all of a sudden its Moonset at the cookout with English Elements: Scent of Success seasonings, good on steak!, of course, cig? The Big ZBLT Blowout!

OG, Blackberry, Kushy.

Chapter 8

CASE SPACE

It was on a Saturday made for early waken bake. Ideal was work'in as a detective on his own case, For chiefly, Little Fox, with the Plyasmx fuel corp. Using Connect A Dream Consolidations, on the Fruit Tobacco, Bud Baby, n Honey Weed case. (of a buzz, if a daze, n daze'inger) which we're geared for the Flight they we're on, him and Agent Spicken, Spicken Span, Agent Nick Span's brother (kandyer). Nick's Middle name Burn, with middle agent Febie Banosea, he should make a profit on this one, as he ran into Raydar Love! (as in Noodle Hit, the first episode of The B.S.-Mind) (the Back Side of the Mind)

Ideal: Hay hurry up twist quick, agent 000's com'in, Rapa Wapa Bapa the only known 000 agent, He's so mean after the fight there's nothing left of the other guys, in the blurry struggles they would simply disappear. Goes by Rapa Zapa.

Potential Confirmable

Relocation complete including SDC, it was another Royal Warmth in the galaxy, yes Zab was to Depart to Zon, but surely not but yes, we've invited him back, he said he'd come. It's the BS (back side) Coming on after the commercial, Zag city was a memory.

Remembering passing Tunea on the way to D Pizza: CUBE to S*P*Y*C Yes Micro city was in the Bush mountainsides full of Rainbow Candy Static Zesty Relish, 00714 GSB Slide'in.

P.S.BS yes Band in Space, they want to come return, as 69 BEATS.

Munch Anticipation

Welcome to:

This is it Oh

Episode 1-Oh

Another cup of coffee, Maybe...?

Maybe not I'll... I won't make it...

This is it Oh!... To many Another one...?

Yes.

E. 2-Oh

This is it!

That's what you think! (flash burn)

Not Green Dig!

Green Dig I'm light'in.

I didn't bring any.

Could pass it?, you fight'in?

You win, just for a bit, hit?

Just for a bit.

This is it Oh...!

Estimize Karata Ware Curator Usually Instinct This More Power

OG Chessy Green Cracks again and again

Reaper

Sorcerer

Ghoul

Creature

Pusher

Done

The End Form

Cook'in down on Tunea (in southern Zon space) with anastral attache, was always a "Treat n Pleasure", the Glade Shade Caramel Grape, quite a calm atmospheric phenomenon, that is good has.

The BS Mind First Episode

Noodle Hit AJV

A leaf in my Tobacco Joint Venture

000.001

As he Drewaly scrutinized the wet ice that glistened above the liquid of his small drink tak'in Him Further n Farther, he noticed 2 colors, the light (yellow) n dark (blue), and the neutral Red, he Had Inscendisation (Image Fixation) an Up to (you) in Feel So Slow (without) with A Loose Be (B) Down at the Tight Fast On. The fragrance will hit your noodle, Resinated End, for Operation "Baby Flower".

CUBE: EL Dopeo... Major J, Munchie Man... Buzz cat... somebody come in over, we need Pizza Delivered to CUBE! Oh yes he has His job back.

Don't Space Your Space Cron, Excuse me, Space, Space Cron Ua-

Edit 4:lla 10.10.22 Tye Wildncool

Chapter 9

Hi (high) God, Genie, Wizard, Spy, Dealer, Effection effected effectively. Were off
to Zon n Tunea Sweetestness.
Supplied by Pluck Truck Inc.- Supply on Demand Corp.
Seer
Man of Knowledge
Shaman
Ranger Dreamer Scout Tracker
Warrior

Song and Gong to Bong
Warm up the tele for the show!

Pack yer Purple Clown Space Star Bunny: (smoke), to be a Royally Happy Love
Monster.
Hookah
Bong
Water Pipe
Pipe
Joint

Grab it J Bud

Yes L. J. (the boss was go'in Atomic on him).

It's burn'in my fingers!/ You work for me!

Yhaw but I'm the only one.

"Wrap n Zap" Financed by D-Pizza, Far Dig-urns are in this week, we are tem-porarily out of Nerve Nourishment. _-The Empty Saddle n English Powers-_<">

ORDER-UP

*5:25/ 717/18 11 17 18/ P.

The Another World E. 2. 7:25

Nondipy

pic

To the Gorilla Girl Itself Girl Scout Cookies Bubblegum Skittles- ovenless Meerschaum Moon Cloud Day.

I better go Yakys com'in over today to clean the coffee maker, you only live twice.

2*Hawaiian Husky,

Telepatics 6

Radio -5

7 Kinesis

'TV-%

1 wonder

1:57.11.10.18p

17 y10m 12 w 4D 1H 32m

Tai Wildncool

New Bak'n Fry at D Pizza then Sven again!

Handmade inc. Ink

Know Aware of the Pizza makin Knobots

Fraternallity on Order

pic

First Boat Ever by Man & God

10:52.12.26.00

1:44.11.26.18

11:00p*Formula-1N2-HHMLB-Grab it J Bud. Yes L.J. (the boss was go'in Atomic on him) It's burn'in my fingers! /You work for me! Yhaw but I'm the only one "Wrap n Zap".-11:08p.1.11

5:20.p 9.6.06_1:00.a 1.11.19_12.Y.4.M.4.D.7.H.40.m_.-"<-_-*!"!*-_->, Financed by W.Z.11:21.p

D-Pizza Far-Dig-ums are in this week, we are temporarily out of Nerve Nourishment. 11:30p
<Barry White Blue Dreams Mango K Doe-Si-Doe>
The Empty Saddle n English Powers/«<WM*0*MW»>\ ...11:08p.1.13.19

12 Morning of 14
T.W. 12:15 @
Edits
Tai Wildncool
Edited 321 by Tai & Jen

To Nick Mason from Tai—

See ya on April 5th—Here's something to check out from the #1 drumline in the state (IN) in "75" at AHS (Andrson High School) a rudiment like, maybe #27,

repeat and repeat very very fast eventually it will bounce + flow vibrating like a roll, cool beans.

D Pizza Bake N Fry

100 Live Fly Coverage Race

1:01.-1:04.4.5.19

I think your last concert on Sun. when you played 5 shows in NY and 7 in LA, in LA me and my brother drove a green chevy van with friends from Phoenix to LA, where we had been going to college ask roger waters who that Fuzzy haired dude was when you all took your intermission, he walked out the South exit area to look at the crowd in the hall maybe, I was standing less than 10 feet away on the other side of a little wall quitly 4-7 min I preformed in school constantly (good instructer) –John Meman

A second episode of

ind

The BS-M 007.867.

MARYJANE

(Bonus story with details-)

Should'nt take long to clean the window out here. Wonder why some woman's getting dressed In my room? Opp's wrong window! I-wow she- she really looks smart in those panties!

Mcnoodle was out to float without a boat, gonn'a write with his mind, need'in ship to shore Communication.

Mcnoodle then knew not what was in store for him on this new case, it could be the end, or a Totally new beginning as he received a phone call that Saturday at 4:20pm about a woman in need He was a professional.

This is my new book, its Murder, a Mystery!

Is she?

I can't tell, all I can tell is she looks pretty, pretty dead! She's been lay'in there twitch'in and I'm Afraid to check her out, she"5-might be like a wounded animal ya just don't want ta disturb um. Course She could just be hav'in a dream!

I don't know what happened, I was just giving her a massage when she started spas'in! You should'nt have lit that up!

I think shes com'in round

Can I hit that?

What's you're name miss?

Maryjane!

Yes it is, do you have a name?

Maryjane!

Pass it to her will ya, how'ed she smell that? Her nose must be Bionic.

Hay it's starting to rain Mcnoodle.

Just what we need more pain. Miss are you in pain?

Maryjane.

Well if you're in pain.

How can she be, she's done hit it three times!

Maryjane!

Just keep hitt'in it miss Maryjane.

Yes I know, she's cute hu?

She is! She's ravishing and I'd like to ravish her!

Dam Mcnoodle!-1 think she finished the smoke.

Good then she'll quit cough'in!

She's on her feet an gone to the restroom.

Mr. Postman!!!

Oh excuse me darl'in did I leave the door unlocked?

What's the postman do'in in there.

He said he had to use the restroom miss.

Maryjane.

What's that she was smok'in?

XP3.

Cause she's out an twich'in again the cherry berry sugar fox!

She was smok'in XP3 before the massage. Help her she's my muffin cake, love pudding, sugar bean, Maryjane everyness!

Nougat Nug

What?

N Gorilla Girl Glue! That's what'XP3 is, should be good. What's she do'in. Miss? Miss? (I knew right Then I was out to travel her mind, it's come to rains an rainbows and I love her rainbow!) Miss!

Maryjaine!

No, on time for that. We'll call you Wildfox.

Maryjane!

Com'in right up. To the Lab for Glueberry, Bruce Banner!

Time for a News break

Why is Green Gold only available at D Pizza, it's like their bringing it in from a different planet Additionally at the Pizza Pub, Miss Pickleberry threw another Hungu Mungu with her mind use'in think Sequence at their sign again in protest.

(Yes Ideal and the band made that other stop at D Pizza coming back from

Zon and bringing A Daze'inger Zon Cron mixture called Green Gold, we're all better off)

Moore Pass Span

IBLT

Ideal

Bouqet

Lickinness

Taste

With the missing Party at the Party

An Ancient Alien Fighting Technique

My Rit's of Wrote's

The Solution to the Answer;

Evacuate, I'm go'in to blow chunks!

Garden Glory update me!

Yes N, something was in his Bourbon!

Yea?

Yea Alcohol!

Mcnoodle!

Don't call me that!

Even as I suspected, been speak'in to her mind again a!

Yea I said you live in her, and I love ya both, then I can back here to smoke more Cronic. That's it I want him out of our misery!

Yes N, you heard him! Out! To the hooter Scooter in space Buzz Boy, to go to the Star Cluster Above the night time eastern star to Zon.

Or at least get me a D Pizza.

Yes N, You heard him Mcnoodle!

Yes I heard him, don't call me that.

1.0.2.3. This is Agent 786, I need a D Pizza-, Yes I'll hold-…

** * * */<">\

Hello this is 8 ..6..7. reporting in!

86-7 is that you?

No! 8-67.

Come on don't play me 7, last time we had you ageing as an agent we talked toyer mom and she Was'nt easy to control, at the time she did have a dozen reasons you might have gone over the hill!

This is Agent 8-67, 8..6..7.

Did you say? 86-7

We're not communicating!

You boys need to get together on these reports!

That's not what I mean by communicating!

Oh wait a minute Agent 786 is he're with us ordering pizza will you be in for a pie, who are you?

Live in Memorex, once or twice upon a time of the future in the future, you're Will makes

Your Dreams JQ the Joint connection!

Thee End

iDEAL will return as Lefty Spacecloud at the Cough Coffee Cafe with ICC (ice cream cake) and Miss Happycrab, it's a dangerous mission!

69 Beats are Officially B.S. (Back in Space).

(Ban-Oh-See)- Do you have any Zesty Papers from the Peppermint Pepper (Indian Smoke) pipes n Papers for the valued 4B J.T.?

10:50p 12/26/00

3:26p 3/20/22

21Y 2M 3W 30 15H 34m

/"<JERRY-_" _-LEWIS>"\

By Tye Wildncool

Cube- Connecting the Worlds

Iboga

The Iboga Tree, the original Tree of Life from the garden of Eden in Genesis, that will make you live Forever, whose leaves will heal the Nations, it can stop heroin addiction.

Cube Policy- If ya can't remember then don't forget!

Holy Spirit- Eats with who he chooses.

Sins against the Holy Ghost will not be forgiven

Chapter 10

N-Nicole Tell me about this L.I.P.G (lost in place grip) Thing and what's happened with GSB?

Nicole- He's been listed out of our control again! This is bad news... While boating ideal Fell asleep after Nugs n Rum and wrecked his boat stranding him him and uzona on a deserted island.They eat a lot of fish and bananas, the good news was he had some marijuana seeds and he planted. All lone and not much chance or hope of becoming rescued as they had waited on the plants which were now harvestable. And would'nt ya know it the next morning they were awaked by helicopters and marching DEA agents! He's back!

N- So you've been eating a lot ua bananas? Well can ya get me an extra Shroomy, D pizza? Get the spotted ones! Ya know I never heard of spotted mushrooms on a pizza, you Nicole?

GSB- Ok yes I was going to D Pizza later no problem.

N- How do you afford going to D pizza all the time?

GSB- I just do!

Nicole- I ate some spotted mushrooms last week sir.

If you ever find yourself in a L.I.P.G, you'll need a Fab-er-J

For many of the trips to D pizza Ideal and the band with their women would bring Green Gold, Which would be easy because it can come from either planet (zon or earth).

For many trips to D Pizza Ideal and the band with their women would bring Green Gold, Which would be easy because it can come from either planet (zon or earth).

Soon to be code named the Lawn Cron case.

Banananana was up at the peace desk of the Older Young, passing out Zap cookies to N and the AM. 00786 and 00867 we're there for a meeting with the Tuneatators (the visual overseers of the universe) and the FBY (federal bureau of yours), (they monitor all marijuana consumption), about Green Gold, they were talking about Blueberry and Bubblegum prouductions and how they might be involved. Ideal knew they were getting close to him and Kandyer and how they were involved.

(the meeting was restarting). Snuff um or Buff um we got to get down to business. D Pizza seems to be the only place you can get Green Gold, and being the only place, it's getting to be a thing...

Now being Lefty Spacecloud, he was trying to arrange his thoughts to meet up with the gang at the Cough Coffee Café with some ICC (ice cream cake) to get them ready to understand about the bug they found at the top of a lamp at home, and how to use it to their advantage, to trick the Tuneatators into believing they were making the move with the seeds after their 8'oclock High, smoking down their joint to a stash Roach at 8pm. When they will have previously moved stuff out to a moving van a little earlier that evening disguised in moving uniforms they swoop with their crew from the van. Leaving the crew to be found later in the apartment by the Tuneatators. The gang was working with Frank from Blueberry and Bubblegum productions, and Gon from Zon who works with Zab personally.

Ideal was jarred from thought by an "Unstable Advisory" why is the locked main door propped open? Who was the last on in?

Guard-Gon!

Gon! Their out there in the car again right! They know it sets off the alarm.

Frank- I think they are at the side of the building that's blocking the wind, I'm going out there I'll get the door!

Yes frank! you do that, your all getting wrote up again.

There is that aphrodiasic smells coming from the office again, ad Ideal they seemed to take an interest in you and Kandyer.

Ideal- Yes Interesting N!

Zab was coming, him and Ideal were going to try to get ahold of this Tuneat-ator thing.

to celebrate their going to do another ZBLT Blowout and Zab was bringing the bacon! Vapor was work'in with PSYC to do the meal for a SPYC Meal.

At the time of the meal, it became time for the Prize drawings. Frank was the winner! accept the Unstable Advisory they were having was the theft of the Prize, 4 Kilos of Green Gold. Things were looking back again, Soaro was up in the air. Vapor was about gone, Sugydrawer was out of place. And Honey Love had a sour look on her face. Then, we have an announcement we have a new Prize, 4 Kilos of Golden Green! Goldren Green where did it come from? How did it get there? And where was it going? Because their always out! Some real loud Dank RDL only available at D Pizza! Exclusively.

Here on Tunea they haven't found it. Growing it all at the spot is where its grown right under their noses! Green Gold grown on Tunea. It's the rich tunea soil. It's their new project!

Note from taste, "Yes traveling above the road is tight"

12:24 am

4/14/24

6:24 pm

Squeezekake productions

Remember save the Whales and the Roaches

Tye WIldncool